THE FALLACY OF THE POEM IS BEAUTIFUL

BECAUSE

IT IS ALREADY THE EMBODIMENT OF A

READER

AHSAHTA PRESS

BOISE, IDAHO

NEW SERIES #56

ORANGE ROSES

LUCY IVES

AHSAHTA PRESS

Boise State University
Boise, Idaho 83725-1525
ahsahtapress.org

Cover design by Quemadura
"Faded Beauty (Greenpoint Windows)," 2012, by artist Barb Choit.
Image courtesy of the artist and Rachel Uffner Gallery, New York.
Book design by Janet Holmes.
Printed in Canada.

LIBRARY OF CONGRESS CATALOGING-IN-PUBLICATION DATA

Ives, Lucy, 1980–
Orange Roses / Lucy Ives.
pages cm. — (The New Series ; #56)
ISBN 978-1-934103-43-2 (pbk. : alk. paper) — ISBN 1-934103-43-8 (pbk. : alk. paper)
I. Title.
PS3609.V48O73 2013
811'.6—DC23

2013021595

CONTENTS

"approached the window as if to see
what really was going on";

GEORGE OPPEN, *untitled*

THE POEM

The fallacy of the poem is beautiful because it is already the embodiment of a reader, presaging the eventual arrival of a realizing eye:

This arrival is a certainty embodied by the figures of the landscape, in their *déshabillé* and witness thereof, in the refreshment of the stream tugging incessantly forward . . .

Yet, as he sues to convince Woodhouse, under these
conditions "no dependence" can be placed on what "Keats"
has said, for upon returning to interrogate Keats in time, one
shall discover only "not myself" in his place—

Thus has the name, "Keats," as "Character," been relieved of
duty: Keats has no "Identity," therefore no relation to which
his name might conform;

Thus, also, the letter-writer's questioning of the legality of his
own composition, " . . . where is the Wonder that I should say I
would ~~right~~ write no more?"

For the vision of the artist arises from illusion, in the form of an illusion, with illusion as its base: illusion is therefore

Returned, demoted, to an identity with itself. Art does not represent the "*Wahrhaft-Seiende*," but rather points to that which cannot imprison truth.

Or, as ordering, in *The Sonnets*, does not have to do
with "chronological . . . development," but instead, with "a
pause," and "[b]alance and a sense of humor about himself,"
the fact of "cut[ting] up" already serving as a metaphor (for
life)

(in its own right)

IN SONNETS

Don't fret they
Knitting her up said

Turn one over for
Away
See your engine was
Where you hurt me

Avoid corners
Good this is the season for it

Knot / occasion

What luck others enjoy not
When I labor when I labor not

All this hell on the other
Side of a little act
Does

Did not believe in objects for when I did
They
Frightened
Figured / competed / located

Why did I never bother putting a name to it

The place from which it asks for

Things may I have some water a plate a jacket

How it retires before the television

I could often feel but did
Not coincide / when I was

If I arrive late this is because I work
On tension of earlier
Demand my last tactic

To have a face with color in it

Gold with some
It was a rumor another

Remembers a refrigerator
Door and getting near
A carton

Seal up my eyes

Try saying Lure

My former I am waiting
That you change back

One fool hopes you
Soften

Know how others think
Look they get letters in
The mail look they're sealed

No dream morning up on shingles what
Pretty part from dream what

Yellow draws one to the street

This is the season bees die

Afternoon the light in the walls
Gets aware of cold on the porch

This is to tell you my new home

How right here becomes
A thing you could have seen

Girl with her trousers rolled
And the bums sit like that

A bee's interest is like a thorn

Everyone's life must be
Rarified some way

Jay with a peanut
On wires
Turns his eye at
Me like an eye
Printed on money

Saying
If you weren't already in
Bed with your pride

And a bang from the
Squirrel's foot each
Time he crosses
Stars in his eyes

From shock from
The treat of it

EARLY POEM

The first sentence is a sentence about writing. The second sentence tells you
it's alright to lose interest. You might be one of those people who sits back
in his or her chair without interest, and this would have been the third
sentence you would have read. The fourth sentence, what does that say, that
says something about how I genuinely feel, even if it no longer matters how I
genuinely feel, that has not even become the topic of another book. The fifth
sentence says that that was left by the wayside because it was such a variable
thing. That's what the sixth sentence said, and says, that it sits there still,
varying, changing its colors, etc., the army of ancient Rome marches by, they
think it is some sort of tomb and display their eagle insignia. The seventh
sentence ill conceals its surprise that I should have tried to make it all look
so far away. The eight sentence is therefore a meditation on something close
at hand. The ninth sentence is a means of approach. In the tenth sentence I
discover I am staring at a list of things I have done written in blue pencil on

brown paper. In the eleventh sentence I draw a one-eyed duck on the paper beside the list. In the twelfth sentence I circle one of the numbers on the list and I start to feel nervous. In the thirteenth sentence I realize I have chosen something. In the fourteenth sentence I decide I will read my choice aloud. In the fifteenth sentence I stall by saying the words "I don't have a choice." In the sixteenth sentence I stall again by thinking about the obelisk on the Upper East Side in Central Park and how it is called "Cleopatra's Needle," and how around the base of the "needle" there are metal supports in the shape of crustaceans, I think they are crabs in fact but sometimes that word is slightly obscene so I consider not writing it. In the seventeenth sentence I think some more about the kinds of joke that employ that word and whether it is worth thinking about such jokes, as it does alter the genre of what you are writing if such things are allowed to be thought as a part of it. The lawns of the park were very green in summer, and it is early summer right now, right as I think to think this, and this is the first time I have lived in New York City for a full year in ten years, this is what I tell as the nineteenth sentence. In the twentieth sentence I recall the list and resolve again to look at it. In the twentifirst sentence I misspell twenty-first with two "i"'s. In the twenty-second sentence I look down at the list, I have circled no. 18759351 on the list. In the twentisecond sentence I misspell twenty-second using an "i" again. In the twenty-third sentence I read what is written next to no. 18759351, it says, "He was sitting on a bench . . . ," but at this moment a breeze enters in through the open window, lifting the page and you begin reading another line, the words, "And you hand in the application and it takes three months and . . . ." In the twenty-fourth sentence you can see me set the page down as another person walks through the door. I turn off the electronic typewriter and scroll out the page and place it facedown on the desk and I cover it with a notebook you weren't aware was also there on the desk. Now you can see it, it is almost the exact same color as the surface of the desk and now you can see it. These were the twenty-fifth and twenty-sixth sentences, respectively, it is the lot of the twenty-seventh sentence to have to announce that. In the twenty-eighth sentence a cloud passes over the apartment on its way into space. In the twenty-ninth sentence, I think, next year this will be the number of my age. The thirtieth sentence is all about the speed at which time is passing. In the thirty-first sentence I won't care anymore, I'll see that reality only accrues to itself and does not have to mean something. In the thirty-second sentence I want you to agree with me. Things happen by chance, and what Montaigne pleads with us to believe, in an essay, is that fortune makes herself known in the act of reading, there is much that I could not have intended which is yet here, I forget exactly how this goes, this being the thirty-third sentence. I sit down beside myself in the thirty-fourth sentence and say to myself, smiling, even small numbers are big. This is the working of time, the thirty-fifth sentence joins in saying this, too, once one has crossed the years their number does not matter. But what I was trying to get across was, I think in sentence thirty-six, that maybe you could not have done things earlier, maybe it just was not possible in those days for whichever reasons. You spend the thirty-seventh sentence attempting to spell those reasons out. You fall asleep, and in the thirty-eighth sentence you dream about a room. The room is a classroom in which you are alone, says sentence number thirty-nine, the windows have been left open and a sentence can be read on the blackboard. In the fortieth sentence you have to force yourself to go on. Descartes's dream, you remember, in sentence forty-one, provided a quote supposedly from Ausonius. This is the forty-second sentence, *Est et non*. Then I think it is safe to say that something begins to happen, sentence forty-three tells us. Sentence forty-four says that you should forgive. Sentence forty-five says that you remember this number as having been particularly beautiful when worn by your mother.

Sentence forty-six says the figures move away. Sentence forty-seven is a sentence about what loneliness names itself in the paradoxical presence of others. Sentence forty-eight says it has a name. Sentence forty-nine says that I cannot remember this name. Sentence fifty says that I go back and try and live there in that moment when I was saying the name. I say, "Happiness." This was sentence fifty-one. That was sentence fifty-two. Sentence fifty-four is a sentence about how there is too much of so many things, there is too much of all the words, but the world runs on underneath them and I keep on imagining how you could have heard me, how you could not have heard me. Sentence fifty-five is a sentence about picking up the phone. Sentence fifty-six is a sentence about picking up a small cellular phone but not using it and willing the phone to ring on its own. The gray cotton of the sweatshirt I wear is a warm cotton in sentence fifty-seven. In sentence fifty-eight I decide to keep on saying the numbers. In sentence fifty-nine I hold the page up to the light and see the type on the other side show through. In sentence sixty you start to believe me. In sentence sixty-one I start to go back to the beginning. I wonder if I should worry. The world is full of pauses, the world is full with continuations, says sentence sixty-three. I let sentence sixty-four go. In sentence sixty-five it occurs to me that I concern myself here with something that ought not to be touched. Sentence sixty-six is a guess that this is the mystery of counting, that is goes on and means itself without having a meaning. I count the people in the distance I can see from my window in sentence sixty-seven. In sentence sixty-eight the breeze has a sweet smell. In sentence sixty-nine, it turns the last week of May in the year 2008. Sentence seventy concerns the lack of what I wanted, in my own mind, to be saying. In sentence seventy-one I'm going so far as to ask you if you can see this, how much of what I thought lay before me remained in the distance. In sentence seventy-two there is a hill there. In sentence seventy-three we see flowers open their faces and then black snakes slide down the face of the hill. In sentence seventy-four there is still nothing. In sentence seventy-five the moon changes place with the sun. In sentence seventy-six this takes place again, only now it is day. In sentence seventy-seven it is still day. In sentence seventy-eight it is still day. Why do you think about tragedy, sentence seventy-nine wants to know, since it is the least likely thing to happen. Sentence eighty will eventually come to me and want to know what I am doing with myself. Sentence eighty-one reminds me to expect this question. In sentence eighty-two something changes. I stay up two nights running and in the morning the sidewalk seems to rise up and meet my feet underneath my feet. Sentence eighty-four contains the question, didn't you already know that this would start to happen. Sentence eighty-five agrees. When I start to read sentence eighty-six I discover it contains the words, It is also true that what you said could *be*. For this reason, sentence eighty-seven is a sentence about why there are certainly points of correspondence between what we expect to be the case and what is. Sentence eighty-eight proclaims it feels the excitement and not the work. Sentence eighty-nine takes action without saying anything first. In sentence ninety I cover my eyes. In sentence ninety-one I uncover my eyes so that I can look again. In sentence ninety-two I cover them again. Now I am speaking to you. Now I am speaking to you. Say the words after me just as I say them. What it means to live is the subject of sentence ninety-six. You are moving out of earshot now. We are not going to miss each other. You have an excellent memory. Please never forget I was the one who told you that

PICTURE

One man's insanity, smell of
His sweat where he comes
To drink in the shade

The hanging face
Whining, and quiet, every
Few minutes—some hungry
Birds overhead

White heels on his sneakers

Like a cat can
See things out of order

Most obvious—most difficult
To remember

A young balding man in blue
Airline socks and
Short tie with a photo of
An eagle came into
The church yard holding the
Hands of two women

He said
"Why aren't we
Singing?

the red boxes drawn over
the limestone face of
the boy's school

the red boxes of tulips

"I thought she wasn't even
going to be sick that
long," said a woman
[next to me] into her phone

a short woman in a
blue plastic coat

a pair of shoes with
shells sewn in

on sale shirts open like
roses cross the floor

there is a woman
kneeling in a black scarf

sunglasses on tables
cards & kids' novels

"I hate it when people look
backwards, I'm like
Look up! Look up!

A girl with cell phone pressed
To her gray and red face
Cries, "But she already
Went and did it!" Her
Eyes like diamonds, big
And square

The man with white dust on his
Hands in the train flipping
His phone shut and then
Open, and sleeping then

The lean man in a jean
Suit with the words
"PIPE WORKS" printed across
The top

The man next to us

Shaking his head, his
Single diamond earring

"I'll call you, I still need
To have lunch

2 rubber bracelets
At his wrists
Pale dragon and crosses

A cup of orange drink in his
Left hand; the flag on a string

Clear plastic cone

The cup of flame above
The refinery

Red floor of the landfill
By the yard of red and white
Cranes

Violet clouds
White plains

above the cement sides of this
highway are tree tops

the U-HAUL headquarters was once
the town hall

docks and crates break apart

below ads in which two muscular

children hold glass bottles

Gray curl of a helicopter

Plastic lamb

Crows

"As long as you don't think
About it like work, what
You're doing is probably cool

"Fuck it looks like Seattle, like
Vegas, both
Together

Pigeons across

Translucence of a setting lawn

Pretzel broken
Open by someone's feet

"You can't see so you
Gotta just throw your hands
Up and hold yourself
There

Brown cellophane
Tugged from a
Crushed cassette tape

Red parallel the iron
Track and comes past

Buildings

EUROPEAN

Yellow-red

Roses at a blue gate

Boys brush aside sand

Orange roses
          White,
          Red

EARLY NOVEL

riding beside the soul in a great
automobile

fences spiral up whatever's
at heart

a face that doesn't look like
a horse

but thinks
with spurs

---

in estimation of the moment before impact
the weight in it rides out but not on legs

the wheels farthest in back lock
and swinging over ice are

muscle under weight of bone
or limb that whips along an arc

---

if one follows one's understanding rather
than resisting: pleasure.

though, not following pleasure:
receiving its press from out

the world as one

enters farther

---

in the economy of appearance
for so many hundreds here

to enter yet
control

just now
your partnership

I love you, giving up
love you, passing in

---

don't we just want to climb
back in our bed

sleep, exchange
imperial, the perfect

rose, nothing
no one's

he remains, the
greatness is in him

and in leaving, the left
is great

absence of emotion in a room

letting us wait

why wait

---

made

and made the flame at least with these
eyes in mind

memory

made night for remembrance

made the intentions that someone wear
them

made water that
it lie in the sink in an adjoining room

passage for carrying

the knot so language would have
mention

of what it later did

the conversation of one
thousand dreams

occurred
a tent fell

---

from the roof of two
mouths, hung there like

the roof of their own
house rocking during

the light
earthquake

the idea there
is a world

and each person
under that tent, another myself
or the wiser picture
of foreigners walking in a field

if we approach
one thinking

it is a child
we haven't

---

walking backwards I said, Tell me
what man is

CIRCULAR NOVEL

The person we dream of is always alive.

Pacific scent of salt, then ivy

I want to ask her how, how she does this

We climb mountains in parking lots

I look at her rayon-blend pants

And want to talk about my vertigo

She turns, she puts the camera on me, as

From frames, I rise, fearing lightly

Thinking of that body in
Another place

Thinking how the wish
Comes around and asks
If I still refuse it

How I refuse and follow
Logic to its hot ends

How the car raises its
Headlights

How riders inside
Arrange their hair

How the slow road
Addresses its driver

A world in which there is no mirror
A world for which there is no other

Highway, life's continual shade
Of entering, doorway

Along whose tunnel, beneath whose ceilings

Without whose screen,[1] there's no remembering?

---

[1] *Wait,* I say, touching her hand

Address another with no screen in mind

And in a place beyond the eyes

There's a wooden man, a man
Of string, he sings to us
Along his legs, re-fashioning

The air, he hears —?

Permanence a lesson a very sweet abode
The itch that circulates beneath the skull

Taking handsomely from us

Well, didn't it all come mercifully up
Against me then?[2]

---

[2] I open my eyes again, she is leaving the room

THE COMPLIMENT

See, the theory this lady has—she's kind of like you, I don't want you to be offended—is that people are not separate, in a general sense. Which means, according to her, there are no, I guess, individual people, just, "ways." Manners and incidences. Remember what you told me? How you said, "That girl is only interesting because she is friends with you"? I used to think about that because I was unhappy, like tell myself it was me, like you said

CATALOGUE

I

The body of water a particular time of day resembles   (*candida*)

Permanence, residence, desire, history, possession   (*culture of*)

That difference, disproportion
Was written in the stars

> *(form of an animal, unnamable*
> *ages point to point, how*
>
> *he rushed to*
> *hunt me with*
>
> *a bluff)*

Il trompe son monde

2

The man next to me appears

Like an angel enamored of

The apple, to be

In redness, as of love

3

In this black underwear or smiling. Teeth long as a beard
or grinning. That there might be less question of favor

In light of the neck's miniature hair. On occasion of envy
and admiration. In hopes of return

Respectfully posed for catalogue photos. With apparent concern for
the passerby. Without impatience

That the song continue to their advantage. Palely

4

The way this teacher crowds up over the woman's shoulder! *Ich?* She asks him warmly *Ich?* The bronze animals twitter, walk on each other's shoulders. They were a statue from Bremen, I tell you, a statue!

5

They lay in bed; more honestly, on the floor; most honest, nude on the carpet under a blanket except for their socks. Behind their heads, a window, and birds rush up it. A clear day, and this is just after the flock passes, she asks, "What?" Literally, he has been telling her about a man he believes practices magic. He is trying to explain what he will do with his life. "My friend," he says, "would not even let me read the book. I tried to pick it up, and he knocked it out of my hands." He says, "It's because he thinks I might be predisposed to do evil. Nietzsche," he says, "though, is only talking about bad and good. There's a difference between bad and evil." There is a large silk scarf stretched across the ceiling. They are on the fifth floor. The authorities these people report to are different. For example, she says, "You look like a cat." For example, he says, "Interesting." At eleven o'clock they rise. He moves toward the closet where he removes a small leather pouch and draws something gold out. "This basically expresses who my father is," he says. He has a Mercedes symbol on a chain in his hand. He does it up around his neck. "I think I am going to wear my cowboy shirt today," he says. She goes into the bathroom. Splashing sounds, faucet and toilet, can be heard. In the meantime, he busies himself with the cd changer. She comes into the room again in a hurry. She draws on the long dark coat he admires

6

Our amazing bed is the future. Do nothing but lie down on it. Owners
love the feeling of weightless sleep

7

Our amazing bed is the future. Do nothing but lie down on it. Owners
love the feeling of weightless sleep Miracle on the inside. Our amazing
bed is the future. Do nothing but lie down on it. Owners love the
feeling of weightless sleep. Miracle on the inside. Our amazing bed is
the future. Do nothing but lie down on it. Owners love the feeling of
weightless sleep. Miracle on the inside. Our amazing bed is the future.
Do nothing but lie down on it. Owners love the feeling of weightless
sleep. Miracle on the inside. Our amazing bed is the future. Do nothing
but lie down on it

ORANGE ROSES

In a kind of fantasy in which I frequently indulge, I discover a way to become so interested in work that I no longer speculate in the negative about the emotional lives of others. In other words, I give up paranoia in favor of business. To actually accomplish this, by which I mean, in life, would mean becoming the most American poet of all time.

In order not to despair, I have to first imagine the day then execute.

Jacques says, "Philosophy is comparing different kinds of philosophy."

I dream about an elevated walkway. A converted ruin. I keep wondering, is it relatively harder to live in the United States now than it has been at other times, and on what grounds could I even make this assessment.

I was trying to remember the numerals "5 3" because I needed to keep a code in mind while I went between screens on the "Droid Eris." I realized I could not think of a single discrete event that occurred in 1953.

Transparent philosophers; it's a sentence about their activity.

I lend Zachary my copy of *The Basketball Article,* by Anne Waldman and Bernadette Mayer. I don't expect it back, but he returns it within a month.

It is sometimes like there are two possible descriptions of the social event, generally speaking: one in which the individual despairs; one in which the individual, as such, is obviated.

I write a poem:

> I just let the flowers die
> I was a terrible person but I didn't care
> Being a person is a specific kind of art
> If you knew me you would know why I am
> Telling you
> I am in the greatest actual comfort
> When I shift my pleasant game
> To the interior
> Where it is right now
> THWACK is the sound a racket
> Makes in a shittier poem
> But we're not indoors
> This is just a voice
> Which makes it sound like we are indoors
> And there are far fewer
> Natural noises now
> It's true than if
> We were anywhere else

This feels like what Dara means about the fascination of "real life," or what is "based on a true story." In this sense, all my desperation (flailing) and plans, the attempt not to do nothing, are also an invention—and therefore not the necessary precursor to some real act.

If I want to do something new or progress, I have to travel farther into a style I have already established. I may at this point add detail. In this sense, the work becomes a fiction of perspective.

I would like to write a story about a person who is continually transformed, who is a woman and becomes a donkey, a cat, a plant, a pencil, a mote, an old woman, etc.

An interest in what seems to be the case precludes my accession to a purely fictional form.

Current technology: IF a representation of reading, THEN legible. IF a legible representation of reading, THEN a caricature?

He spoke to his wife. He told her not to hit herself in the face. He said that she should not be hopeless, that she could not be hopeless. She had too much to live for. If she were a great writer she would never have had these thoughts. She said that she did not know what she should do. He said that it was easy, that there was a choice, that she was no longer five years old. She silently wished to herself that she were five years old. She silently felt as if she were five years old, and all the world were still ahead of her, every literate thought and act.

For me conceptualism could be something like, "Write a 1200-page novel set in 1872, detailing the travels and observations of a French novelist in the North American countryside."

List of various details:
a. A click
b. A wooden peg
c. Black saliva
d. Dizzying shine

I notice the poverty of my own writing during a reading and feel intense regret. Do I become like those I parody in my prose to Sam? I am "just" like them?

A memory from a wedding: I congratulate the bridegroom on a "beautiful ceremony," and he grimaces, plastic face thinly muscled over.

Rousseau: "J'ai vu de ces gens qu'on appelle vrais dans le monde."

The scene in Buñuel's *The Phantom of Liberty* in which a sniper is sentenced to death and then released by officials from his handcuffs: He shakes hands with his lawyer and lights a cigarette, descends an elaborate staircase to sign autographs in the courthouse lobby.

One student has written that he does not understand why he was not permitted to bring his "philosophical ideas" to bear in his paper.

Something we talk about yesterday evening: If one is a witch, it is because (i.e., it would be because) one can (could) turn people to stone.

Quality of time. One wishes to assign qualities to it, but then these are the qualities assigned; planned and not discovered. Why should the unexpected be of such value, when we are trying to sense not it but rather that in or against which it occurs?

The human could in fact only be transfigured through imitation?

I meet with Julia, who remembers me as "Canadian," or "Kim Deal."

In a dream Peter is in front of an ocean. I am transformed into a bunch of daisies bound with orange string.

I make a list of numbers and cross them off as I finish pages. The numbers do not correspond to an actual projected page limit, but act rather as a prop to make venturing into prose bearable. I tell myself, "You will not have to keep doing this forever," which, of course, I won't.

1928 letter from Williams to Zukofsky: "...virtue exists like a small flower on a loose piece of earth above a precipice."

I find a stanza from a poem I wrote when I was 23:

       Yellow-red

       Roses at a blue gate

       Boys brush aside sand

       Orange roses
             White,
             Red

Why on television it is always clear which is the "right" person with whom to share one's affections?

I remember almost a decade ago Rob talking to me on the phone about stories he was writing about his father. Rob said writing made him want to shop. Could this show how some illogical behavior is more meaningful than others.

Those whom no one loves, live, and perhaps are happy.

I can see that someone cannot quite explain, but she covers her confusion with a weird smile, under which she hides her lack of authority. Now I am smiling.

List from observation:
a. Naturalism
b. chapping in 18th-century pastel
c. treatise on hems, bows
d. symbolical coat
e. mask, or loup
f. shade, tambourine
g. figured damask coat, or banyan
h. Praktischer Anweisung zur Pastellmalerei
i. 1792

I go to the gym and spend 50 minutes on the treadmill and elliptical machine. I watch television. Wanda Sykes tells Ellen about her grapefruit-sized tumor (she is 47). I do some sit-ups. At the supermarket the checkout girl tells me about the time she wore "really heavy pants" and a white t-shirt in the rain.

Reason is a language. In this sense it is no more or less perfect than other languages.

I walk uptown to 36th for an opening. Ben's painting (of the Italian flag with a bucket over it) has already sold. Later on the train he tells me he spoke to someone our age who has no hand but only a thumb at the end of one of his arms, "I shook his thumb." If I also had such a thumb this is what others would say of me.

Maybe I have a boring way of treating life. I watch a man across the street throw cardboard boxes at a second story window.

Language, since inorganic, is not suffused by time and does not "die," despite the expression. And yet without the depth of time, the possibility of sequence, there could be no meaning.

Have lunch alone with Sam because Christian doesn't show (cannot get out of bed). For some reason Sam humors me. I say something about how useless is the term "fiction."

List of events:
a. They discover a beetle in milk.
b. Flaubert critiques the pious death of a child.
c. A drunk slips her phone into a toilet.
d. Someone paints a roof to look like snow.
e. A fuchsia bud.

The present is whatever must be alleviated by a message.

At a lecture I make no effort to take notes but rather withstand my boredom by consuming it, avidly even, as if it were a broth. I find that later when I am outside on the street I have begun to dread the possibility that I allow a sort of lust for passivity to overtake my life.

In a dream I ride to a village built in what I privately term, "the Austrian style." I die and walk along a sunny highway.

It's not simply that you become "depressed," that is far too inexact. You can forget how to do a thing, how to make the gesture that accomplishes your desire. You forget to try to reach whatever this or that may be, because you generalize. You only reason with yourself, you make no attempt. There is in fact no way to justify this sort of behavior.

In a dream I am with someone I love. I enter a café made of unvarnished wood; diners sit single-file on enclosed balconies with rugged plastic windows.

Plot:
1. A white scratch.
2. Emma pauses near a smudge.
3. Orange roses wrapped in hair.

I find a fragment, partially highlighted:

This is the sense in which people speak of art as "doing," which is to say, confusedly. Anyhow, sometimes one has hunted successfully in the wreckage that constitutes her fear

I imagine it as a point in time that is also a view, smeared laterally and with no regard for the artificiality of the gesture, and here one might "feel" (apprehend) the affections of the artist.

I think about how in the end it is true, something that we see in other people, or what frightens us, is death, possibly our own, or just a sign of it, like, in another personality. This is at any rate what threatens me and makes me fear, rather than love, others, if I do. What is curious is that these sensations or affections never happen in a single moment, which is to say, never take the form of an event. That they forever manifest themselves in this strange otherwise, a present that isn't "happening," is what seems to make it impossible not to agree to go along with (i.e., feel) them.

1994. Six dresses by Rei Kawakubo. Bias-cut silk skirt, paisley, tie-die, attaches to t-shirt. Cold skin of the model. In verdant shade effected by topiary. Laceless work boots in glossy black calf, fawn interior, tongues in grass.

I seek the approval of others often, and less often others, or some others, recognize I do so.

In a dream I enter a store selling lamps from the 1950s. Porcelain. Californian cream/white.

I have humiliated myself so much and am not even famous. Or: the humiliation of the non-famous is basically unreal.

In a children's book illustration a female figure rides on the back of a bearded monkey and cats scatter in her path.

Why is it writers are so much less good than they once were? Is it possible that it is more difficult than it once was to speak of life, which is to say, a life, as a whole? Obviously we understand that there is living and death, but there is a very little idea of a formal (which is to say, cultural) relation to either one of these states. This is very American. People are like their parents only on account of obsessions, since there is no way of living, only "lifestyle." A given period has no symbolic value.

I read somewhere that Keats's statement about beauty is about ambition.

I sometimes look younger than I am and sometimes older. There is no sure way to look one's age. To look one's age, one would have to know what one's age looks like, and this no one really knows. I suddenly remember a day in Berkeley when I was on a residential street and a man walking the other way turned and slapped my ass as I passed him. And I went to work in lush abundance.

During a time of waiting, a lot of things won't be apparent.

I spend several weeks trying to write a summary of a famous novel and end up with a single sentence that has nothing to do with it:

Somewhere it's possible a statue sails through a thin floor or the limb of a tree is mistaken for a fist of marble; intervening leaves shake as if with delight, a rancid jelly.

Ben is sick and has been reading Louis L'Amour. What is the first example of the "American aesthetic" as purveyed by Europeans; could one locate this in certain objects, texts. What would such an argument look like. The political cartoon of the segmented snake, for example.

I have never known how to write poetry. It is not a question of relating language to a person one is but rather of relating it to the exact person one is not.

A stanza:

It's not that this is a feeling opposed to
Or distinct from others
This, Lucy, is feeling
This is the knowledge of feeling
You are smart
You are slightly intelligent
It is like a mastery of self
An art
That you will die in

BEASTGARDENS

FIRST GARDEN

Beastgarden.

SECOND GARDEN

Bees go mad on late summer evenings, should
People stray from their jobs towards water

Beastgarden.

THIRD GARDEN

Who makes the rented red boat's
Oars turn

Who is the younger one always
Turning up

Who professes to be better because
He is just looking

Who says he is worse off as
He cannot look

Beastgarden.

FOURTH GARDEN

The unicycle girl, thin
Like one with a sexual problem,
Goes through
The Schlosspark. This follows:
Father rolling his eyes

Beastgarden.

FIFTH GARDEN

The man from Manchester
Has my breast in his hand

These are funny
They don't do anything do they

Being burnt by a fire I say

Beastgarden.

SIXTH GARDEN

Similarly, if only
You grasped some
Titanic misery or a
Love like an old man's

Beastgarden.

SEVENTH GARDEN

Where were we

A ballroom competition goes on
A yellow satin bikini
A fuchsia floor-length are
Dancing; an audience is
Drinking, clapping 1 2 3 1 2 3

Beastgarden.

Carrying a bucket full

Of a broken window or

Watching people and their mirrors on

Tv; the hollowed-out woods tamped down

By snow; air

Passes from purple to blue into a

Black pitched lower than

Trees;

Losing the key, breaking in

With a spade, sliding on

Down to the floor to the front

Door as every evil or only

The brass of familiar luck.

If some surface would hold

Our hopes then show them to us.

A world never does much

But get stranger.

There are loops in the sky

And towers for radio.

Wherever we go

I'll still be able to say

Something. I'm calling

On you who enter

In the loveliest thing

Thinking ever cut.

But it's not in history

Or the first person, so

Let the lyric stop.

Black trees shake against fair

Strips in the night.

Many thoughtfully placed

Yellow deck-lights.

Fireplace with a mouth of fire

And two swinging eyes.

An iron cat under

Ceiling fans. Blackbird feathers

Near the largest pane of glass.

Listen to thermostat. Watch

A new telescope

Train on far-off hill. And

All around small blankets

Made by hand from wool.

Much is imperfectly

Divided.

To know how to get really

Good and safe is

Useful

For being good. Then

Enter the mistress, the table

Where the meat stood.

Couches absorb screen-light for days.

The most important thing

Was time, and

Along it our little

Brain, jeweled, red.

There was how we lived, then

How we dreamed we lived.

Traveling underwater,

Returning in a streaming herd. Where's

My banquet and where is my sword?

The moon's face opens to the day

Just and only here.

ON IMITATION

My understanding of writing was for a while informed by an idea about insufficiency I got from America. Take images and compare these to words: Words suffer. Consider the naturalness of the photograph, its informative, absorbing detail. It is even possible that the photographic image resembles nature most on purely analogical grounds, since nature is often understood to have no insufficiency in its "bounty."

But here I only hint at what I take to be some of my earlier errors. To explain:

Somerville, Massachusetts, May 2000.

I was sharing a house with two other people the summer I was 20. The floor of the room where I stayed had been painted white and was warped, sloping southerly. I had recently found an edition of Anne Sexton's poetry in a box on the street and was reading it because I had heard of the poetry of Anne Sexton. I could not understand what I read. I read something by John Ashbery and wondered why he refused to say anything. Someone at the office said put a bowl of water in front of the box fan.

I was having trouble reading. I suppose I was having trouble completing tasks in general, but this seemed, somehow, unexceptional. I was doing a very bad job at work. Mostly I purchased smoothies and stared at guano-spattered chimneys.

I made some stupid lists. The lists said things like, "Read this book. Write a devastating novel of filmic specificity. Write a long, visually precise poem in which you tell the story of a redemptive journey in which the heroine is transformed. Read these four books. Understand the power of John Ashbery. Read each word of *The Critique of Pure Reason*."

On weekends sometimes I lay on the floor of my room and pondered the perfection of everyone's actions. "Everyone is acting so natural," I thought. "Everyone knows just what to do."

Nature was a kind of horizon, a mark.

You said the word "nature," and after this there was nothing more to say. Everything you said next was just words pretending relevance to a far more plausible being.

Emerson calls nature, "essences unchanged by man," but I am not talking about living beings or the planet, all of which probably do not fall into Emerson's category anyway. These were organic, and probably they were part of nature, but actually they were only *examples* of what nature might be.

For me, nature was a category. Nature was that which goes unquestioned; it is whatever is understood to have a right to be.

Anyway, I was only thinking about art: Movies were natural. The higher their budgets, the more natural they appeared. Writing was weak. The 1990s were over yet there was the lingering torpor of Clinton-era aesthetics, the need to have seen *Titanic*, its nasty sentimentality epitomized by Kate Winslet's crimped orange hair . . .

I began to make a list of moments in poems I considered not entirely lost, where language had been appropriately pressed into the service of detail. This was where writing was likeable and moving and important and natural—in its presence as visual detail. I made a list of the best images in the poetry of John Ashbery:

1. "The lake a lilac cube"
2. "green thorns"
3. ". . . he comes in, wiping a block of ice / On a chipmunk dishtowel, his face glittering"
4. "black gingerbread"
5. ". . . the exhausted shepherd / The marble of his Swedish copper forehead"

I considered one of the few discrete, perfectly clear images in the lucid poetry of George Oppen, "a white powdered face."

The summer passed.

I was in college.

Things were not going well.

A professor stood before the lecture hall with several dried leaves of tobacco. She had a runner's body, a goofy face below conservatively dressed hair; word was she sought professional advancement through administrative coups. She agitated a tobacco leaf. It crackled near her clip-on microphone. She spoke about Edgar Allen Poe's Virginia.

It was so natural.

Taking our first exam for her survey of American lit I inscribed what I believed was an excessively relevant example:

I am writing in this book. I am writing in this book. I am writing in this book. I am writing in this book. I am writing in this book. I am . . .

This would demonstrate my command of New Historicism. I carefully offset the text.

The teaching assistant offered me a "D." He wondered in turquoise loops if I would speak with him. He wanted to know what I expected. He said that we could make a pact. His tufted fingers were adorned with multiple class rings.

I had a Hotmail account and owned a Gateway PC. The Democrats were about to lose the election.

The question was not what can words say, but what can they show. Where the word evokes an image, it does some sort of work. But most of the time people are just talking about something or other.

This is to say, I took the photograph to be a very natural mode of expression without even finding unique photographs particularly expressive in themselves; it was just so clear to me what a photograph is *of*, the information it conveys. But what is a word "of"?

The way my theory of appropriate linguistic imitation worked was through pointing. It was best to use words that had as limited as possible a set of referents. Like the linguist Ferdinand de Saussure, whose *Course in General Linguistics* was popular in humanities guts at the turn of the last century, I liked the idea of a picture of a tree hovering over the word "tree." Or: better yet, we should put the word above the picture; the word should produce a thought of the picture; from the thought of the picture we might arrive naturally at the thing; the word should point us in this direction, should do nothing less and nothing more.

I wanted a written language that spoke plainly, stupidly, of *things*. If not like a photograph, light's writ, writing should be, or so I thought, as much like a drawing as possible.

Around the same time I was coming to these tyrannical conclusions about the proper use and form of written language I was, as I have mentioned, going to college. It was becoming increasingly difficult to, on the one hand, hold my experimental beliefs and, on the other, pass the classes I was enrolled in. The most pressing problem was how long it took to write. I would spend a whole day trying to put together a pair of sentences, and for this reason even an uninventive prompt like "Describe some violence in *Coriolanus*" could require almost a week's work.

If I had been smart I would have just studied art. Instead, I quit school.
I used money I had saved to fly to Los Angeles, where I rented a car from a
drycleaners near LAX. It was a red two-door with rims. I took Route 1.

I had decided that I was going to search for the most dumb writing, the most
image-like. I hoped it would be so much more natural.

Moro Bay, California, March 2001.

Crescent City, California, April 2001.

Gertrude Stein once wrote, "Nature is not natural and that is natural enough." There are miles and miles of hillside into which Route 1 has been blasted. I got out of the car and climbed over a fence into a field that had two horses in it. I wandered around small towns and drove into areas of cultivation. On an empty inland road I did 120 and was picked up by aerial radar.

I practiced writing landscape. Repeatedly I stopped the car and attempted to write down what I could see.

I stopped in San Francisco where the car was towed after I got lost in the Mission. I retrieved it from a dusty lot. Seeing it for a second time I realized I had no idea what I was doing. I drove to Crescent City, the northernmost dot on the Californian coast. I turned around again.

I wondered: What is it the novel does that the poem doesn't do?

If any of the writing I did during this time were extant, I would include it.

I'm not sure what happened to the "landscapes," the lists I made of visual detail with very small people and animals and buildings and trees and clouds. I think when I got back to the Northeast Corridor I left them in a notebook, and then this notebook was lost in a move or thrown away. I didn't for a long time know what the point of these written landscapes was, since they had no narrative structure, and even if they did satisfy my desire to have a kind of writing in which each word stood perfectly for a single, real thing—a thing whose name the word was—no one else could possibly want to read this writing. (Some of the landscapes went on for ten pages, nouns with minimal prepositions, adjectives, and gerundives powering interminable anaphora.)

At some point I started taking poetry classes. It's because of this that I even have some kind of written record of my trip/extended exercise. The following poem was, then, composed after the fact. (I never, by the way, became any more natural.)[†]

<hr />

[†] If, by the way, someone asks me what I now think about the list of images by John Ashbery, I will say I think they are effective. If someone asks me what I think about my old theory of writing—why, for example, I no longer write this way—I will say that in the end it was inconvenient. I don't entirely accept the way that I am writing to you now, though if I do write this way, I recognize that with and in a language that precedes me.

I DON'T KNOW

The first and only time I saw
The desert in California I was
Alone. Outside Joshua Tree my
Motel had an entire baseball team
Staying in it; at night
They wandered around the pool
And vending machines with
Their shirts open. White cotton
With thin red bars, a
Blue "C" above the heart

I remember there was a movie on tv
About two alcoholics in love
I laughed out loud. I spent the day
Climbing to the top of a short gray
Mountain. The sky was clear, the moon
Visible at 4pm like paint off
The face of a dime pressed in

"Looks like the ground on the moon"
A French woman standing beside me
Said to her American friend

Driving out of town, my phone
Started to ring. I pulled over
Next to the 1001 Nights Motel

It was my college roommates calling
From Boston. When would I come home
They asked. What was I doing?

ACKNOWLEDGMENTS

Thanks to the editors of *The Colorado Review, Conjunctions, Fence, 1913, Ploughshares, Triple Canopy,* and *Volt,* in which journals these poems and prose originally appeared.

Some poems also make up a chapbook, *Novel* (Projective Industries, 2012). Thank you, Stephanie and Tom.

The cover photograph, "Faded Beauty (Greenpoint Windows)," 2012, is by artist Barb Choit. For her series "Fade Diary," Choit photographs UV-faded printed matter in storefronts, as well as exteriors as they are reflected in window glass. Image courtesy of the artist and Rachel Uffner Gallery, New York.

The epigraph is taken from George Oppen's series of untitled poems, *Discrete Series.* Oppen quotes a phrase from Henry James's "The Story In It."

"On Imitation" was prefaced by the following introductory text, when first published:

> Edmund Burke, in his *Philosophical Enquiry into the Origin of Our Ideas of the Sublime and Beautiful,* has a mysterious sentence, "The second passion belonging to society is imitation, or, if you will, a desire of imitating, and consequently a pleasure in it."
>
> In summer of 2012 *Triple Canopy* editors Sam Frank, Lucy Ives, Christine Smallwood, and Dan Visel, embarked on an inquiry into the purpose of writing. The editors decided that, rather than compose in straightforward critical prose, each would invent a story about him or herself (a story narrated by someone named "I") that would in some way express his or her concerns, doubts, euphoria, and/or opinion concerning the act of writing. They agreed that it would be OK to lie, and that no one should make everyone's life more difficult by writing more than 2000 words.
>
> This symposium or accord, which now takes the form of four short and thematically linked narratives, is presented to you here under the title, "I Know What You Did Last Summer."

AHSAHTA PRESS

SAWTOOTH POETRY PRIZE SERIES

AHSAHTA PRESS

NEW SERIES

This book is set in Apollo MT type
with DIN titles
by Ahsahta Press at Boise State University.
Cover design by Quemadura.
Cover art by Barb Choit.
Book design by Janet Holmes.
Printed in Canada.

AHSAHTA PRESS

2013

JANET HOLMES, DIRECTOR
ZACH VESPER, ASSISTANT DIRECTOR

JERRI BENSON, *intern*   STEPHA PETERS
CHRIS CARUSO   INDRANI SENGUPTA
ZEKE HUDSON   ELIZABETH SMITH
ANNIE KNOWLES   MICHAEL WANZENRIED